HERMAN LEIMBACH ELEMENTARY SCHOOL
8101 Grandstaff Drive
Sacramento, California   95823

The World and Its People

FAMILIES AND NEIGHBORHOODS

The World and Its People

SERIES AUTHORS

Val E. Arnsdorf, Professor,
   College of Education, University of Delaware,
   Newark, Delaware

Carolyn S. Brown, Late Principal,
   Robertson Academy School, Nashville, Tennessee

Kenneth S. Cooper, Professor of History, Emeritus,
   George Peabody College for Teachers, Vanderbilt
   University, Nashville, Tennessee

Alvis T. Harthern, Professor of Education,
   University of Montevallo, Montevallo, Alabama

Timothy M. Helmus, Classroom Teacher,
   City Middle and High School, Grand Rapids,
   Michigan

Bobbie P. Hyder, Elementary Education Coordinator,
   Madison County School System, Huntsville,
   Alabama

Theodore Kaltsounis, Professor and Associate Dean,
   College of Education, University of Washington,
   Seattle, Washington

Richard H. Loftin, Director of Curriculum and Staff
   Development,
   Aldine Independent School District, Houston, Texas

Norman J.G. Pounds, Former University Professor of
   Geography,
   Indiana University, Bloomington, Indiana

Edgar A. Toppin, Professor of History and Dean of the
   Graduate School,
   Virginia State University, Petersburg, Virginia

GRADE–LEVEL CONTRIBUTORS

Kim Eyler, Former Teacher,
   Wyckoff, New Jersey

Gloria Lemos, Teacher,
   McGee Elementary School, Pasco, Washington

Mary Lou Martin, Teacher,
   San Diego Unified School District, San Diego, California

Katharyn Smith, Teacher,
   The Meadows School, College Park, Georgia

Patricia Terai, Teacher,
   Woodlin Elementary School, Bothell, Washington

Map chapter by Stan Christodlous, Executive Editor,
   Social Studies, Silver Burdett Company

FAMILIES AND NEIGHBORHOODS

ALVIS T. HARTHERN   Professor of Education
University of Montevallo, Montevallo, Alabama

SILVER BURDETT COMPANY   Morristown, New Jersey
Glenview, Ill. • San Carlos, Calif. • Dallas • Atlanta
Agincourt, Ontario

CONTENTS

MAPS

END-OF-CHAPTER
SKILLS DEVELOPMENT

A LETTER TO YOU FROM THE AUTHOR

Dear Pupil,

I am so happy you have this book. I wrote it especially for you. It is called Families and Neighborhoods.

This book has seven chapters. In the first six chapters you will be learning how families meet their need for food, how clothes are made, why families need shelter, and many other things about how families live. Some of the families will be like your family. Others will be very different.

In the last part of this book, you will learn about our country, the United States of America. You will learn about the many places families like to visit, about some of our country's symbols, and many other things.

I hope each chapter will be interesting and exciting for you.

Sincerely,

Alvis T. Harthern

My friends and I are quite alike
We eat and sleep and play and hike.
We see and taste and touch and smell
And hear the sound of the dinner bell.

And yet we're really not the same
In size or shape or likes or name.
We each choose different things to do
I like to paint my toys bright blue.

Some friends I know just love to sing
Or skate or swim or read or swing.
Yet same or different, it's plain to see
I like my friends and they like me.

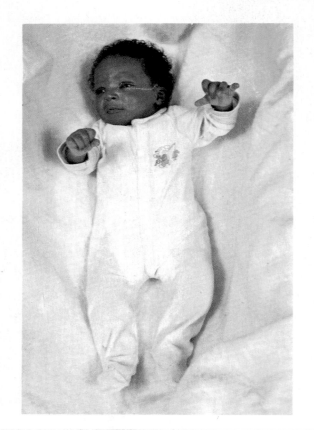

4

5

KEY FACTS

1. All living things need air, food, and water.

2. Living things grow and change.

3. People are both alike and different.

4. People learn from each other.

5. All people have feelings.

VOCABULARY QUIZ

Look at the pictures. Look at the words.
Match the word with the picture.

alike   helper   happy   share   sad

REVIEW QUESTIONS

1. Find some things that are living.
2. Find some things that are not living.
3. Which will grow and change?
4. Who is being helped?
5. Who is the helper?

ACTIVITIES

1. Draw a picture of a happy face and a picture of a sad face.

2. With the help of your family, make a picture time line of your life. Show how you have grown and changed since you were a baby.

3. Draw a picture showing one way you are a helper to someone in your family.

PUTTING THINGS IN ORDER

Living things grow and change.
Look at the pictures.
Each picture shows a different time
in the life of a living thing.
Put the pictures in order from
the youngest to the oldest.

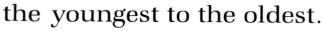

Susy's family is quite big,
But mine is very small.
Susy has six sisters,
While I have none at all.

I have lots of cousins
But they live far away.
All of Susy's cousins
Visit every day.

Isn't it amazing
That these families both could be
The very best of families
For Susy and for me.

The people you live with
are your <u>family</u>.

Some families are large.
Some families are small.

Family members do things together.
What are these families doing?

Where is this family?

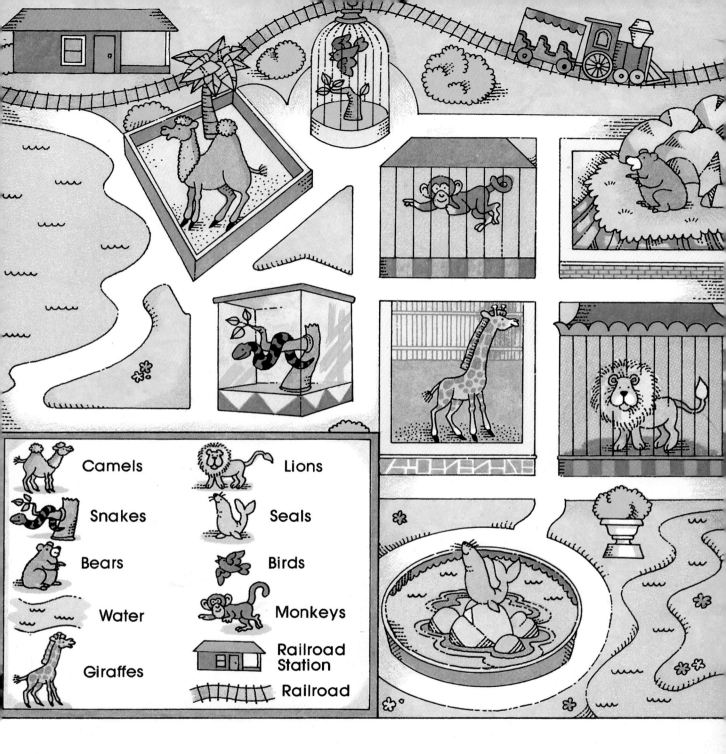

Camels

Snakes

Bears

Water

Giraffes

Lions

Seals

Birds

Monkeys

Railroad Station

Railroad

This is a <u>map</u> of a zoo.
A map can help you find places.

Families <u>change</u>.

To change means to make different.

People work at different jobs.

Do you work around the house?

People have many <u>needs</u> and <u>wants</u>.

Which of these are needs?
Which of these are wants?

Birthdays are fun.

Powwows are fun, too.

What <u>holiday</u> is this?

People learn from one another.
Tell what is being learned.

KEY FACTS

1. People live in families.

2. Families are alike and different.

3. All families have needs and wants.

4. Families celebrate special occasions.

5. Family members learn from one another.

VOCABULARY QUIZ

Look at the pictures. Look at the words. Match the word with the picture.

flag

family

birthday

work

map

REVIEW QUESTIONS

1. Who is teaching each child?

2. What is each child learning?

3. Name other things family members learn from one another.

ACTIVITIES

1. Draw a picture of something you would like for a birthday gift.

2. Bring in a picture that shows something all families need.

CLASSIFYING NEEDS AND WANTS

Look at the pictures. Some are wants.
Some are needs. Fold a sheet of paper in half.
Write <u>Needs</u> on one half.
Write <u>Wants</u> on the other half.
Study the pictures carefully.
Decide whether each is a need or a want.
Write or print the name of the picture
under the correct heading.

clothes

water

ball

house

friends

wagon

food

cat

37

Who made the jelly
In the jar near the sink?
Or the peanut butter?
Or the milk that you drink?

Who grew the wheat
For the bread on the shelf?
If you wanted a carrot,
Could you grow one yourself?

Dozens of people
Work hard just to feed you
To help you grow strong
And to show that they need you.

No restaurants.
No grocery stores.
Think of that!

Long ago there were no stores.
Families could not buy food.

How did people get food long ago?
Pilgrim families grew most of their food.
They also hunted and fished.

The Pilgrims left their homes in England.
They crossed the Atlantic Ocean.

In which direction did they travel?

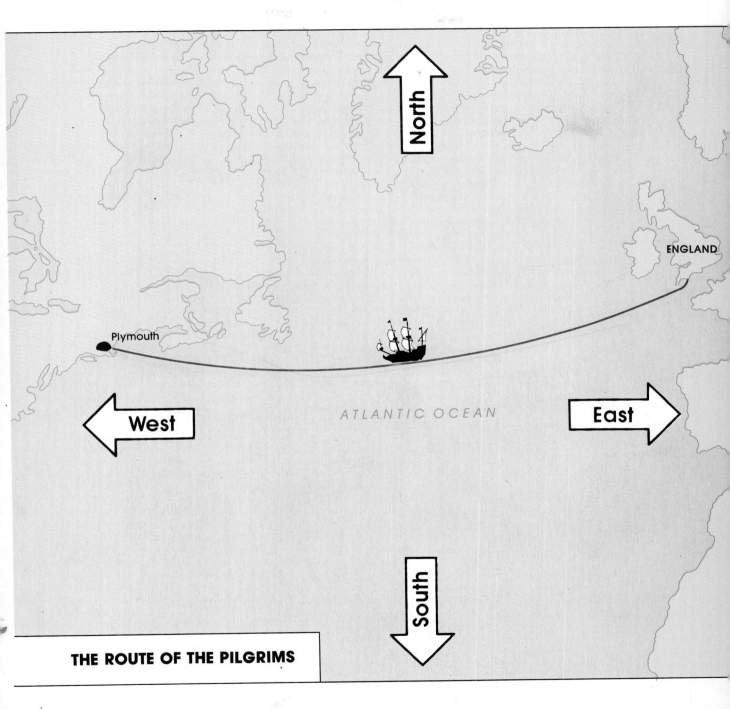

ENGLAND

Plymouth

North

West

East

South

ATLANTIC OCEAN

THE ROUTE OF THE PILGRIMS

The Pilgrims ate mostly these foods.
Is your favorite food shown here?

corn	peas	fish	squash
berries	duck	potatoes	turkey
pumpkin	cherries	deer	apples

The Indians helped the Pilgrims get food.
The Indians were <u>helpers</u>.

The Pilgrims wanted to give thanks.
They made a special dinner.
The Indians were invited.
This was the first Thanksgiving.

Today few families grow their own food.
Farmers grow food for most people.
Some farmers grow grain.
Some grow fruits and vegetables.
Some raise dairy cows.

Farmers work to grow food.
Other people work with food, too.
Can you name these workers?

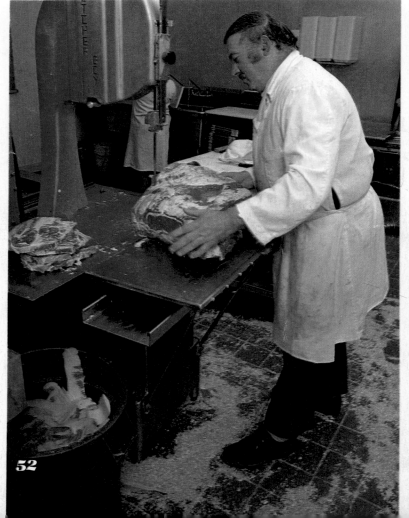

KEY FACTS

1. All people need food.
2. Families today get food in many ways.
3. The Pilgrims got most of their food by hunting and farming.
4. The Indians helped the Pilgrims to get food.
5. Pilgrims and Indians celebrated the first Thanksgiving.
6. Families today depend on many workers to supply their needs for food.

VOCABULARY QUIZ

Look at the pictures. Look at the words. Match the pictures with the words.

fishing
hunting
planting
buying

REVIEW QUESTIONS

1. Who works on a farm?

2. What kinds of food do farmers grow?

3. What do farmers do with the foods they grow?

4. Who buys the foods at the stores?

ACTIVITIES

1. Draw one picture showing how a family got food long ago. Draw another picture showing how your family gets food.

2. Find pictures showing farming long ago and farming today.

USING THE ALPHABET

Families eat many different foods.
These pictures show some of the foods
families eat. Look at the pictures.
Look at the name near each picture.
On a separate sheet of paper, write
or print the names of the foods in
alphabetical order.

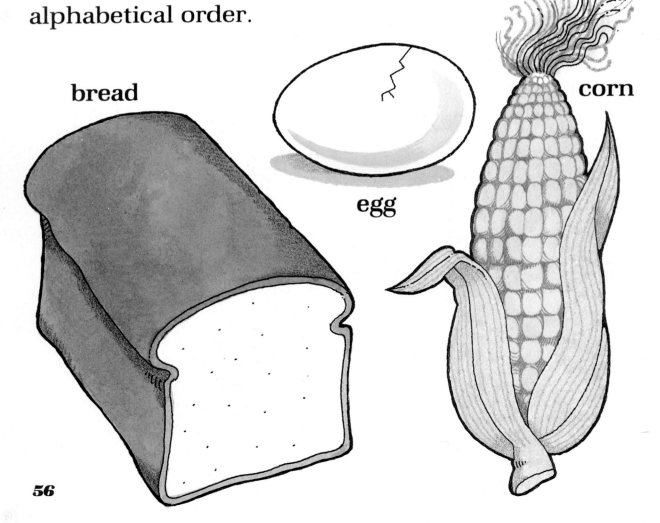

bread

egg

corn

ham

grapefruit

apple

duck

fish

Peter's jacket wouldn't snap,
And Mary lost a boot.
Martin's zipper wouldn't zip
His brand new winter suit.
Hazel's fingers got mixed up
In mittens lined with fur.
It was so hard to wait until
The teacher got to her.
But snap, find, zip, fix
The teacher did each thing,
And promised much less trouble
When they dressed for school in spring.

All families need <u>clothes</u>.
Clothes are a basic need.
Some clothes are for warm <u>weather</u>.
Some are for cold weather.
What do you wear on cold days? On warm days?

All clothes are not the same.
Some clothes are for dressing up.
Some are for playing.
Some are for sleeping.

63

People do not all dress the same.
Different kinds of clothes are worn
in different parts of the world.
Look at these pictures.
What kinds of clothes do you see?
Are the clothes the same?

Clothes are made from cloth.

Some cloth is made from wool.

Wool comes from sheep.

Wool is cut from the sheep.

Some cloth is made from cotton.
Cotton is a plant.

Picked cotton is tied into bales.
The bales are sent to a mill.

Many machines
are used at the mill.
Some break the cotton
into small pieces.
Others clean the cotton.

Cleaned cotton is made into ropes.
The long ropes are made into thread.

Thread can be dyed many colors.

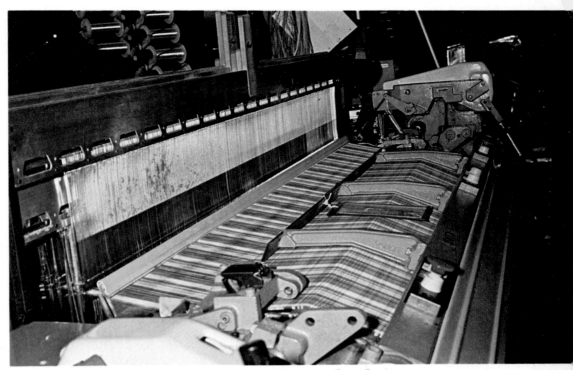

Some thread is woven into cloth.

Cloth is used to make clothes.

Do you know who these people are?

How can you tell?

Clothes help us tell who people are.

Name the people in each picture.

KEY FACTS

1. All people need clothes.

2. Clothes are a basic need.

3. Special kinds of clothes are needed for certain types of weather.

4. Different kinds of clothes are worn in different parts of the world.

5. Cotton and wool are used to make cloth.

6. Uniforms may be worn to identify members of a particular group.

VOCABULARY QUIZ

Tell whether the following sentences are true or false.

1. Cotton is a plant.

2. Wool comes from sheep.

3. All people dress the same.

4. Cotton and wool are made into thread.

REVIEW QUESTIONS

1. In what ways are summer clothes different from winter clothes?

2. Why are different kinds of clothes worn in different parts of the world?

3. What kind of cloth can be made from a plant?

4. What is cotton used for?

5. Where does wool come from?

6. How is wool removed from the sheep?

7. Why do some workers wear uniforms?

ACTIVITIES

1. Find pictures of people wearing different kinds of uniforms.
Have classmates guess the kind of work each person does.

2. Pick a special day or special event.
Make a picture of the kind of clothes you would wear.

UNDERSTANDING RELATIONSHIPS

Special kinds of clothes are needed for certain types of weather.

Match the clothes with the type of weather in which the clothes should be worn.

Some workers wear special uniforms.
Tell what the worker in each picture does.

Tall houses
Small houses
Flat houses
Fat houses
All of the houses I see.

They are there
Everywhere
Just to share
Love and care
With all of the family.

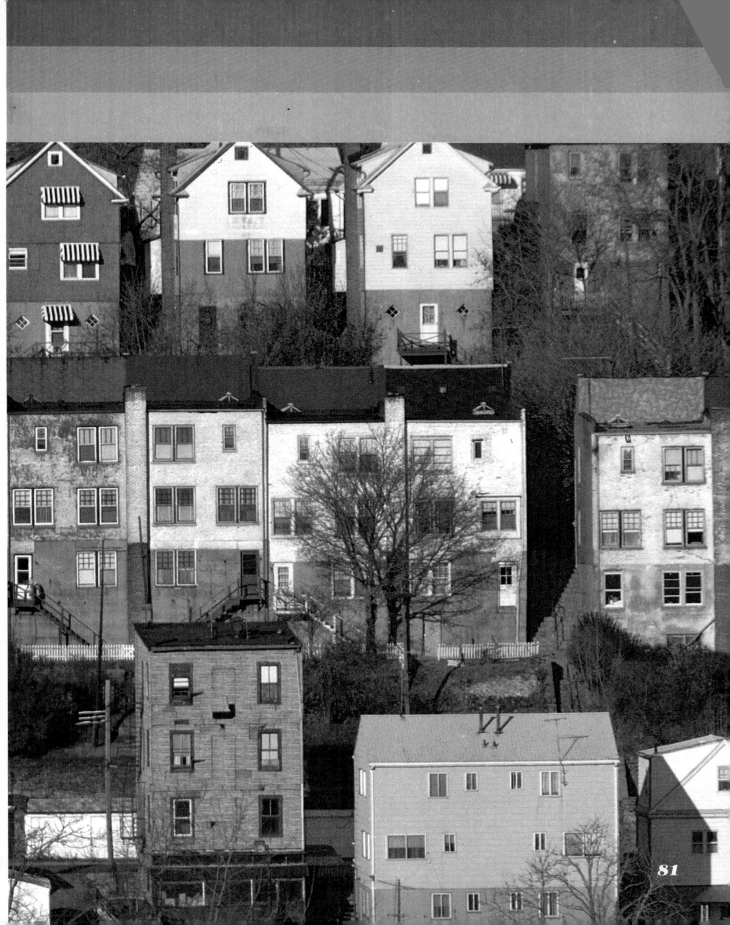

All families need <u>shelter</u>.

Homes are shelters for families.

Shelters protect families from the weather.

Some animals need shelters, too.
What kinds of animal shelters do you see
in these pictures?

Families live in many kinds of homes.
What is your home like?

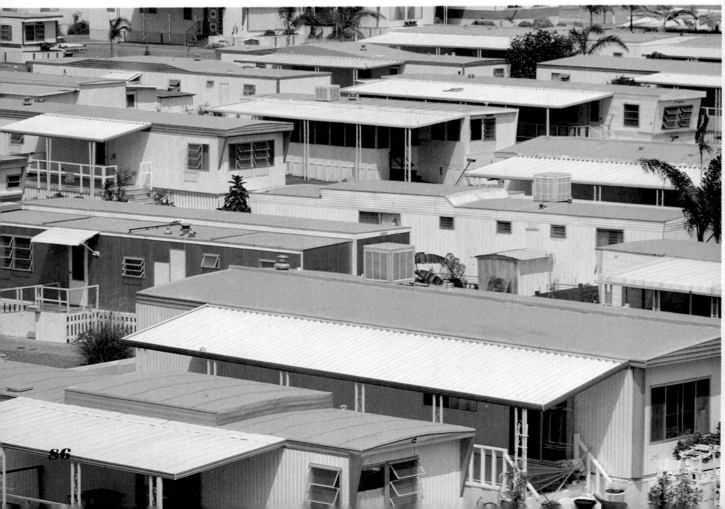

Long ago Americans built shelters like these.

89

Families live in many places.
Some families live on a mountain.
Some live in the desert.
Some live near water.

Families do many things at home.

They cook and eat.

They work and sleep.

They have fun together.

What are these families doing?

Homes change.
Old homes are torn down.
New homes are built.

Let's see how a new house is built.

Plans must be made.

Land is cleared of trees.

Many skilled workers are needed.

These workers are building a wall.

Many parts of the house are made from wood.

This worker is using brick.
The bricks are used to
build a fireplace.

Pipes are put in.
They will carry water to the house.

Electric wires are put in.

Windows are added.

Special materials are used.
This special material helps
keep the house warm in winter.
It will also help keep the house cool in summer.

This worker is using another special material.
This material separates one room from another.

Some rooms need special things.
Do you know what this worker is doing?

This worker is building steps.

Painting is done last.

Sewer lines are put under the ground.

Now the house is ready.

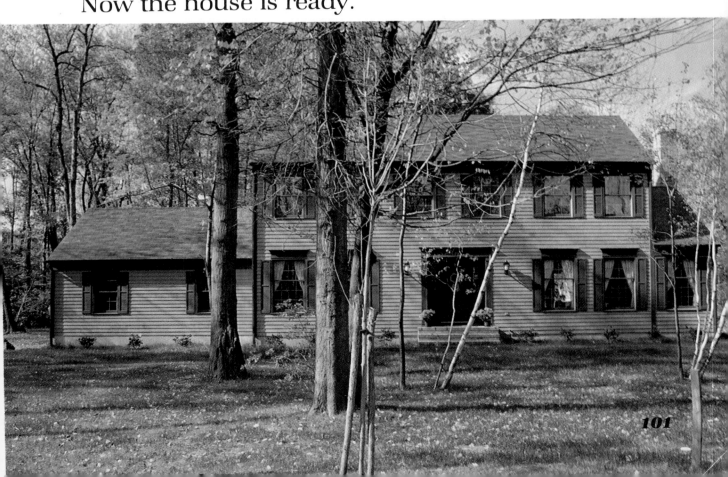

All homes have an address.
Your address tells where you live.
What is your address?

It helps people to find your home.

KEY FACTS

1. All families need shelter.
2. Houses provide shelter for families.
3. Families live in many kinds of houses.
4. Many workers are needed to build a house.
5. Houses are made from different kinds of materials.
6. Your address tells where you live.

VOCABULARY QUIZ

Tell whether the following sentences are true or false.

1. Many animals live in shelters.
2. All families live in the same kind of shelters.
3. Families live in many different places.
4. Different types of materials are used to build houses.

REVIEW QUESTIONS

1. Why do people need houses?
2. Name a type of material used in building a house.
3. Name two kinds of animal shelters.
4. What kind of shelter can many families live in?
5. What are two things families do at home?
6. Why do you have an address?

ACTIVITIES

1. Draw a picture of the outside of your house.
2. Find pictures of families and shelters that are different from yours.

UNDERSTANDING A FLOOR PLAN

A map of a room is a floor plan.
This is a floor plan of a classroom.
Study the floor plan carefully.
Use east, west, north, or south to
answer the following questions.

1. In which wall is the door?
2. Start at the door and go to the table.
In which direction did you go?
3. Next to which wall is the teacher's desk?
4. Next to which wall is the closet?
5. The table is opposite the door.
Where is the table?

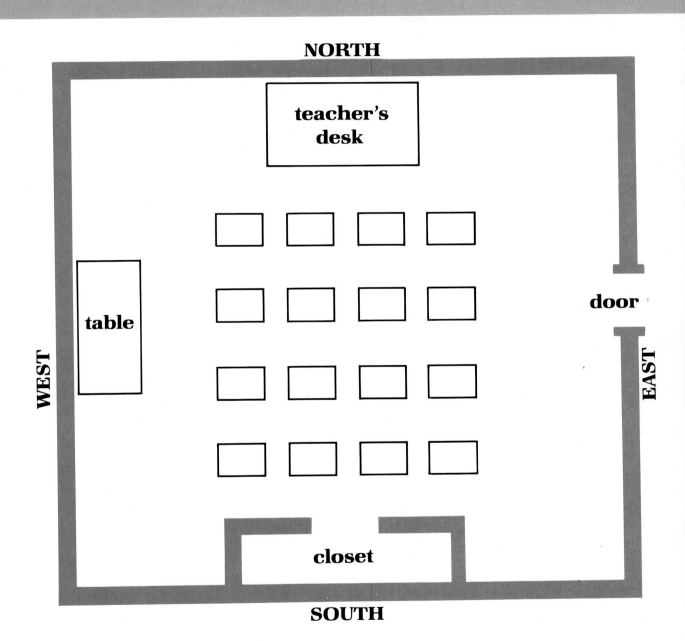

Sally Smith was sick one day
And couldn't go outside to play.
Her neighbor Jim brought in a treat
Some nice fresh fruit for her to eat.
Her neighbor Mabel said she'd look
For Sally's favorite storybook.
Billy called her on the phone
So she would not feel alone.
Poor sick Sally felt quite good
About living in her neighborhood.

Families living near one another make
up a <u>neighborhood</u>.
This is a picture of a neighborhood.
It was taken from an airplane.

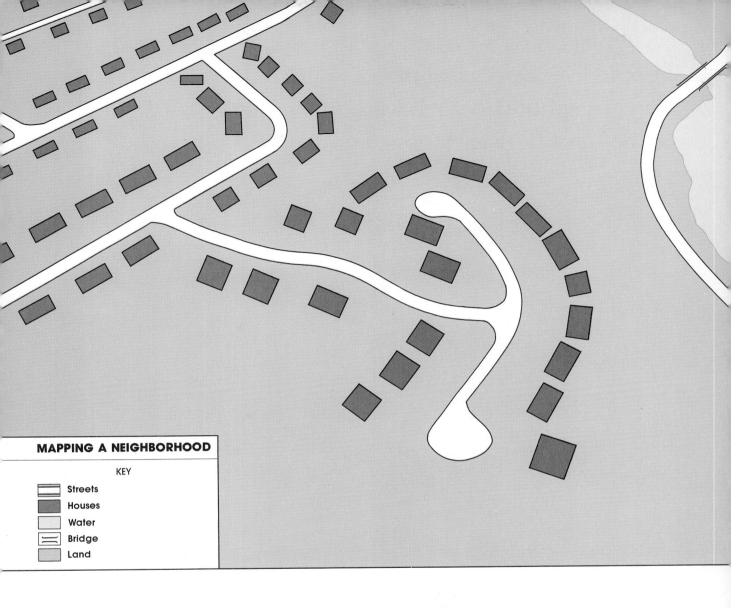

MAPPING A NEIGHBORHOOD

KEY

Streets
Houses
Water
Bridge
Land

This is a map of the same neighborhood.
How is it like the picture?
How is it different?

People live, work, and play in neighborhoods.
Some neighborhoods have only houses.
Some have houses, stores, and factories.

People shop in neighborhoods.
They buy goods. Books and food are goods.
Name some other goods.

This is Pam.
She can brush her teeth.
She cannot fix a broken tooth.
A dentist does this for her.
Fixing teeth is a <u>service</u>.
Who else provides a service
in your neighborhood?

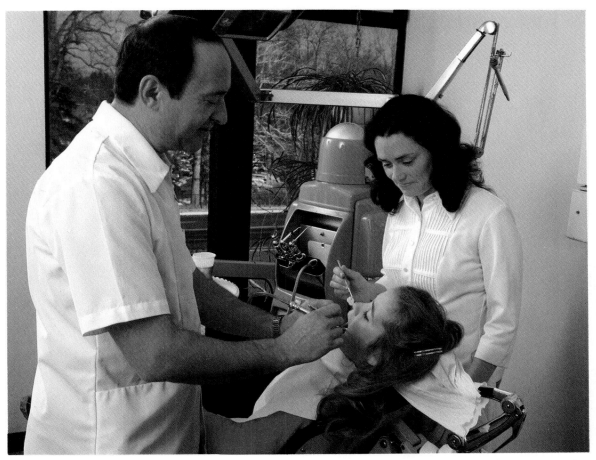

Many neighborhoods make up a community.

Some communities are big.

Some are small.

What is your community like?

117

KEY FACTS

1. Families living near one another make up a neighborhood.

2. Some neighborhoods have only houses. Some have houses, stores, and factories.

3. Families can buy goods and services in some neighborhoods.

4. A group of neighborhoods make up a community.

5. Some communities are big . Some are small.

VOCABULARY QUIZ

Tell if the following sentences are true or false.

1. A police officer provides a service.

2. Food and clothes are goods.

3. All communities are small.

4. All neighborhoods have stores and factories.

REVIEW QUESTIONS

1. What is a neighborhood?
2. Food and clothes are goods. Name other goods.
3. Name two service workers.
4. What makes up a community?

ACTIVITIES

1. Find a picture of a neighborhood that has only houses. Find another neighborhood picture that has houses, stores, and factories.
2. Draw a picture of a service worker or a worker who makes or sells goods.

READING PICTURES

Some neighborhoods have only houses.
Some neighborhoods have places for people
to live, work, and shop. Study the pictures
on the next page. Then answer the questions.

1. What do these pictures show?
2. In which neighborhood can families shop?
3. Which picture shows houses in a city area?
4. Which picture shows houses in a small town?
5. How are houses in the small town different
from those in the city?

CHAPTER 7

Living in the United States

I know a lot about my country—
Please forgive me if I brag,
But I know that it has 50 states
And a very special flag.

I know that it has cities
And towns and farmland, too.
It is home to many people—
It is home to me and you.

I know a lot about my country—
And I want to say out loud,
"My country is the U.S.A.!"
This fact makes me quite proud.

123

We live in the United States.

The United States is our country.

Our country has a <u>flag</u>.

The flag is a <u>symbol</u> of our country.

THE GREAT SEAL OF THE UNITED STATES

Our country has other
symbols.

When we see these
symbols
we think of our country.

Our country is part of the world.

Find the United States on the map.

Canada is north of the United States.

Mexico is south of the
United States.

What ocean is east of the
United States?

What ocean is west of
the United States?

Alaska

Pacific Ocean

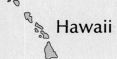
Hawaii

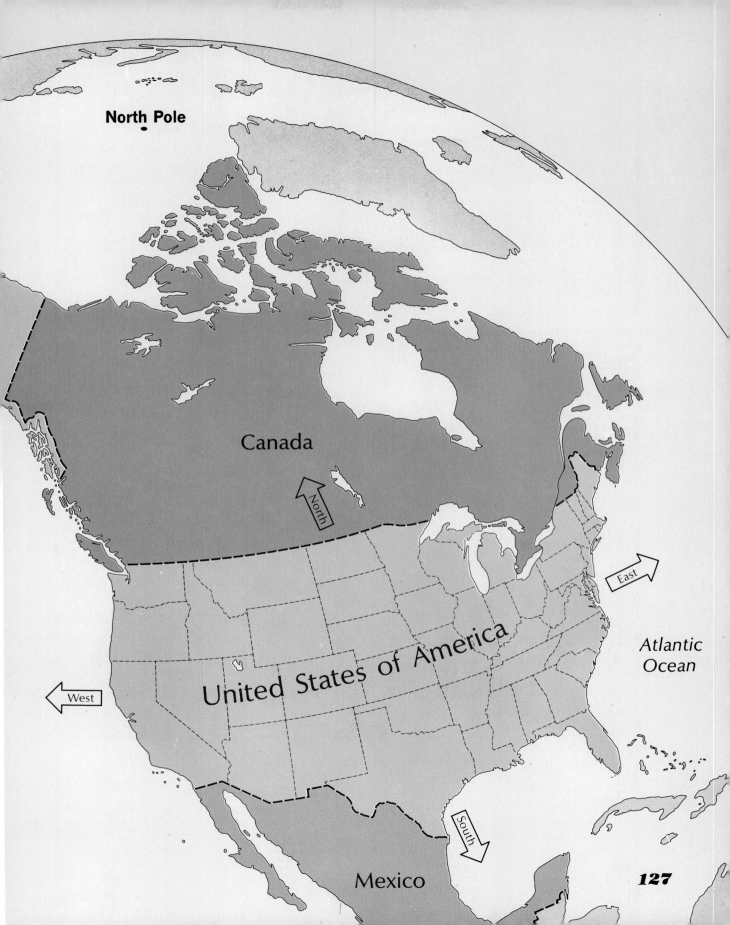

North Pole

Canada

North

United States of America

West

East

Atlantic
Ocean

Mexico

South

127

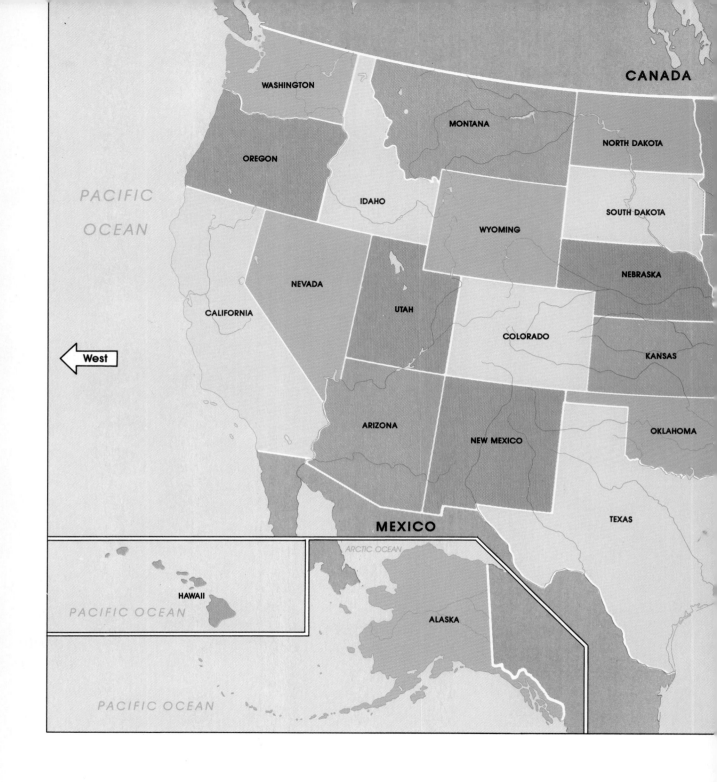

This is a map of our country.
It has 50 parts.

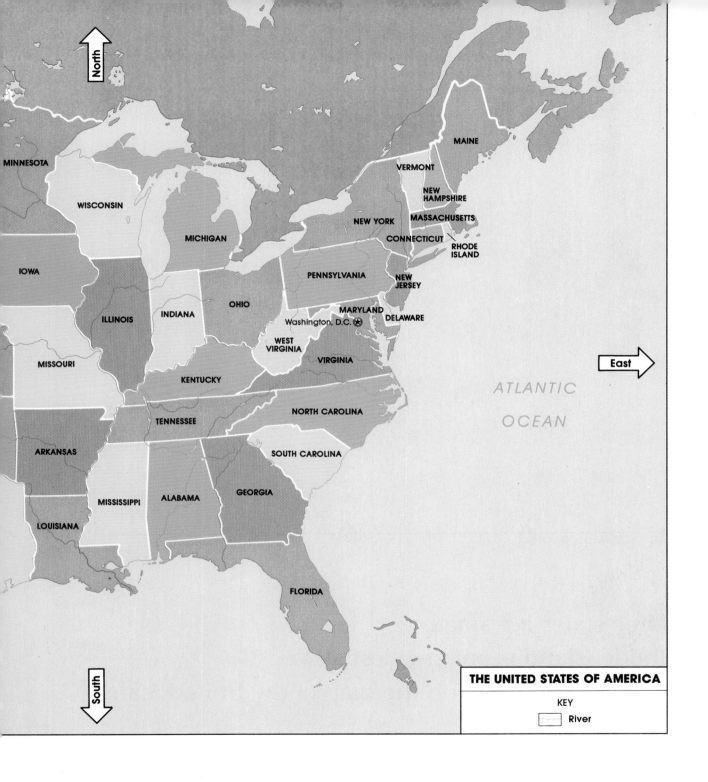

North

South

East

MINNESOTA

WISCONSIN

IOWA

ILLINOIS

MISSOURI

ARKANSAS

LOUISIANA

MISSISSIPPI

ALABAMA

TENNESSEE

KENTUCKY

INDIANA

MICHIGAN

OHIO

WEST VIRGINIA

VIRGINIA

NORTH CAROLINA

SOUTH CAROLINA

GEORGIA

FLORIDA

PENNSYLVANIA

NEW YORK

NEW JERSEY

MARYLAND

Washington, D.C.

DELAWARE

CONNECTICUT

RHODE ISLAND

MASSACHUSETTS

NEW HAMPSHIRE

VERMONT

MAINE

ATLANTIC OCEAN

THE UNITED STATES OF AMERICA

KEY

River

Each part is a state.
Can you find your state on the map?

129

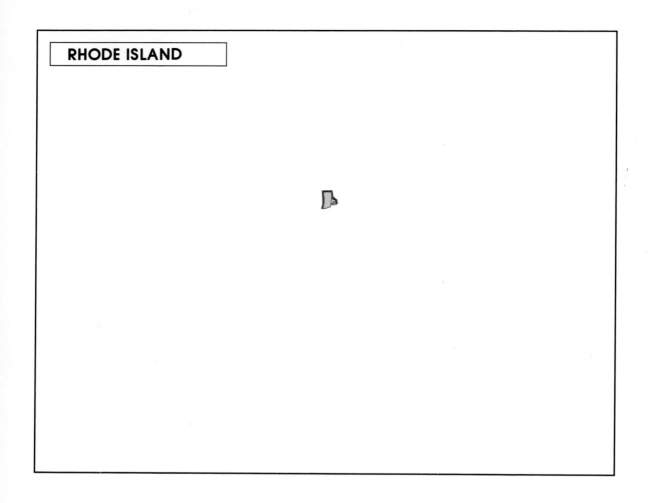

RHODE ISLAND

Some states are small.

Rhode Island is our smallest state.

Find Rhode Island on the map of the United States.

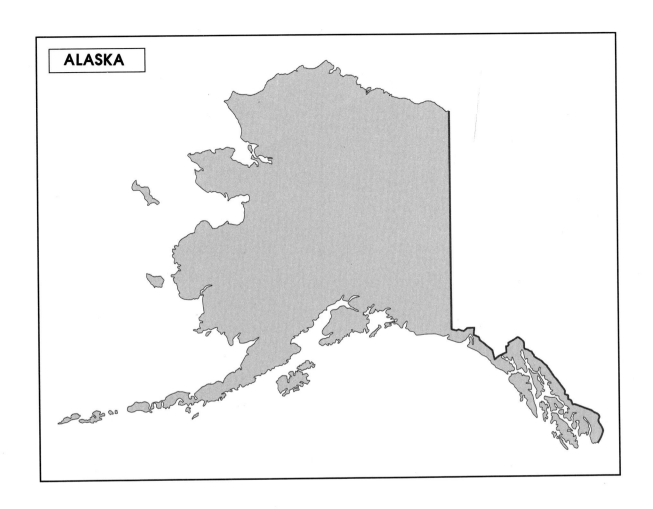

ALASKA

Some states are large.

Alaska is our largest state.

Find Alaska on the map of the United States.

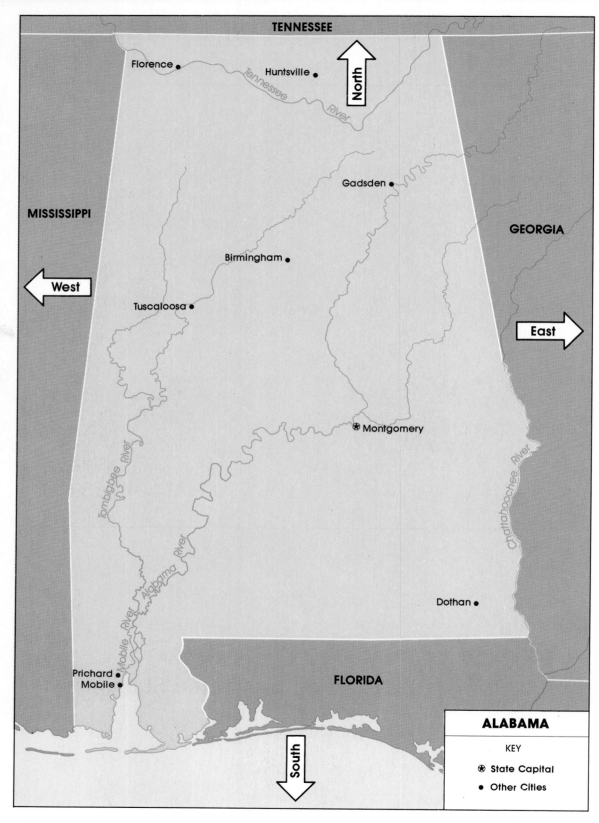

This is a map of Alabama.

Alabama is a state.

It is in the southern part of the United States.

Every state has many towns and cities.

Name some cities in Alabama.

One of the cities is very special.

It is the state capital.

Montgomery is the capital of Alabama.

Plans for all the people in Alabama
are made in Montgomery.

The United States has a special city.

This city is the capital of our country.

Its name is Washington, D.C.

Congress meets in Washington, D.C.
Men and women in Congress make plans
for our country.

The United States is a big country.
Millions and millions of people live here.
They do many kinds of work.

The United States has many resources.
Water and coal are resources.
Trees are resources.
Why are they resources?
Can you name another resource?

There are many places to see in our country.

Families like to visit these places.

They can see what our country looks like.

143

Our country has many holidays.
Thanksgiving is a holiday.
Columbus Day is a holiday.
What holidays do you celebrate?

144

Let's sing a song about our country.

AMERICA

WORDS BY SAMUEL FRANCIS SMITH   TRADITIONAL

My coun - try! 'tis of thee, Sweet land of lib - er - ty,

Of thee I sing; Land where my fa - thers died, Land of the

Pil - grims' pride, From ev - 'ry moun - tain - side Let free - dom ring!

KEY FACTS

1. We live in the United States.

2. The flag is a symbol of our country.

3. Our country is part of the world.

4. Our country has 50 states. Some states are small. Some are large.

5. Washington, D.C., is the capital of our country.

6. Millions of people live and work in the United States.

7. Our country has many holidays.

VOCABULARY QUIZ

Choose the right word for each sentence.

flag   states   capital   resources   holiday

1. One symbol of our country is the _____.

2. Thanksgiving is a _____ in our country.

3. Our country is divided into 50 _____.

4. Trees and coal are _____.

5. Washington, D.C., is the _____ of our country.

146

REVIEW QUESTIONS

1. What is the name of our country?
2. Name two symbols of our country.
3. What country is north of the United States?
4. What country is south of the United States?
5. What is the name of our smallest state?
6. What is the name of our largest state?
7. Name two resources found in our country.
8. What do men and women in Congress do?

ACTIVITIES

1. Find some pictures of places you would like to visit in the United States. Tell why you would like to visit those places.
2. Draw a picture that shows you and your family celebrating a holiday.

USING A MAP

Study the map on this page
and answer the following questions.

1. What nation does this map show?
2. What does the key help you find?
3. In which direction will you travel
if you go from City 1 to City 2?
From 2 to 3? From 3 to 4? From 4 to 5?
From 5 to 6? From 6 to 7?

NORTH

WEST

EAST

SOUTH

Key
City

USING MAPS

Use the map on pages 126–127 to answer these two questions.

1. Which country is closer to Canada, the United States or Mexico?

2. If you were in Canada and wanted to go to Mexico, in which direction would you travel?

Use the map on pages 128–129 to answer these questions.

1. In each of the following, which state is larger?
   a. Louisiana or Texas
   b. Hawaii or Alaska
   c. Arkansas or New Mexico
   d. Indiana or California

2. Is the Pacific Ocean east, west, north, or south of the United States?

3. Is the Atlantic Ocean east, west, north, or south of the United States?

Picture Word List

change

clothes

family

flag

goods

helper

holiday

map

needs

neighborhood

resources

service

shelter

symbols

wants

weather

CREDITS

Cover: Gregory Hergert
Maps: R. R. Donnelley Cartographic Services
Poems: Barbara Thompson Howell

Chapter 1 viii–1: Brian Haggerty for Silver Burdett. 2: Dr. E. R. Degginger. 3: *t.* J. Gerard Smith; *b.l.* © Harald Sund; *b.r.* J. Gerard Smith. 4–6: Michal Heron for Silver Burdett. 7: *t.* Silver Burdett; *b.* Michal Heron for Silver Burdett. 8: *t.* Victoria Beller-Smith; *b.* Yoram Kahana/Peter Arnold, Inc. 9: *t.* Michal Heron for Silver Burdett; *b.* Brian Haggerty for Silver Burdett. 10: *t.* John Running; *b.* Mike Mazzaschi/Stock, Boston. 11: Silver Burdett. 12–15: Maggie Swanson.

Chapter 2 16–17: Victoria Beller-Smith for Silver Burdett. 18: L. L. T. Rhodes/Taurus Photos. 19: *t.* Michal Heron for Silver Burdett; *b.* Cary Wolinsky/Stock, Boston. 20: *t.* L. L. T. Rhodes/Taurus Photos; *b.* © Susan Johns/Photo Researchers, Inc. 21: Michal Heron for Silver Burdett. 22–23: Olivia Cole. 24–25: Silver Burdett. 26: Philip Jon Baily/Stock, Boston. 26–27: Silver Burdett. 27: *t.* Donald Dietz/Stock, Boston; *b.* Owen Franken/Stock, Boston. 28–29: Silver Burdett. 30: *t.* Owen Franken/Stock, Boston; *b.* John Running. 31: Brian Haggerty for Silver Burdett. 32: *l.* Michal Heron for Silver Burdett; *r.* Silver Burdett. 33: Michal Heron for Silver Burdett. 34–37: Maggie Swanson.

Chapter 3 38–39: Milton Feinberg/Stock, Boston. 40–41: Silver Burdett. 41: Eric Carle/Shostal Associates. 42–43: Gil Cohen. 44: Silver Burdett. 46–49: Gil Cohen. 50: *t.* Courtesy, John Deere; *b.* Cary Wolinsky/Stock, Boston. 51: *t.* Terry McCoy/Taurus Photos; *b.* Grant Heilman. 52: *t.* Cary Wolinsky/Stock, Boston; *b.* Silver Burdett. 52–53: L. L. T. Rhodes/Taurus Photos. 53: *l.* © Bonnie Freer/Photo Researchers, Inc.; *r.* Werner Stoy/Camera Hawaii. 54–57: Olivia Cole.

Chapter 4 58–59: Silver Burdett. 60: William Hamilton/Shostal Associates. 61: *t.* L. L. T. Rhodes/Taurus Photos; *b.* Erik Anderson/Stock, Boston. 62: Peter Menzel/Stock, Boston. 63: *t.l.* John Running; *t.r.* A. Majewski/Taurus Photos; *b.* © Tibor Hirsch/Photo Researchers, Inc.© Paolo Koch/Photo Researchers, Inc. 65: *t.* Pier Giorgio Sclarandis/Black Star; *b.* © George Holton/Photo Researchers, Inc. 66: Dr. E. R. Degginger. 67: John Running. 68: Webb Photos. 68–69: S. L. Craig/Bruce Coleman. 69: Glenn Short/Bruce Coleman. 70–72: S. L. Craig/Bruce Coleman. 73: *t.* S. L. Craig/Bruce Coleman; *b.* Silver Burdett. 74: Cary Wolinsky/Stock, Boston. 74–75: J. Gerard Smith. 75: *t.l.* © Henry Bradshaw/Photo Researchers, Inc.; *t.r.* J. Gerard Smith; *b.* © F. B. Grunzweig/Photo Researchers, Inc. 78–79: Olivia Cole.

Chapter 5 80–81: © Guy Gillette/Photo Researchers, Inc. 82–83: J. Gerard Smith. 83: *t.* Herman J. Kokojan/Black Star; *b.* Silver Burdett. 84: *t.l.* Mike Mazzaschi/Stock, Boston; *t.r.* Cary Wolinsky/Stock, Boston; *b.* Frank Siteman/Stock, Boston. 85: *t.* Breck P. Kent; *b.* © Richard H. Smith/Photo Researchers, Inc. 86: *l.* © C. Vergara/Photo Researchers, Inc.; *r.* © Paolo Koch/Photo Researchers, Inc. 86–87: Willinger/Shostal Associates. 87: *t.* © Harald Sund; *b.* Diane M. Lowe/Stock, Boston. 88: *l.* Milton Feinberg/Stock, Boston; *r.* Silver Burdett. 88–89: Katherine S. Thomas/Taurus Photos. 89: *l.* © Tom McHugh/Photo Researchers, Inc.; *r.* Marty Heitner/Taurus Photos. 90: Cary Wolinsky/Stock, Boston. 91: *t.l.* Gamma/Liason; *t.r.* Dr. E. R. Degginger; *b.* Diane M. Lowe/Stock, Boston. 92: *t.l.* Owen Franken/Stock, Boston. *t.r., b.* J. Gerard Smith. 93: *t.* Cary Wolinsky/Stock, Boston; *b.* Joan Menschenfreund/Taurus Photos. 94: Tony Castelvecchi/The Foto Place. 95–102: Silver Burdett. 103: *t.* Elaine Wilks/Taurus Photos; *b.l.* Imagery; *b.r.* Silver Burdett.

Chapter 6 108–109, 110: Silver Burdett. 112: *t.* Joan Menschenfreund/Taurus Photos; *b.* Stephen Voynick/Shostal Associates. 113: *t.* Dr. E. R. Degginger. 113 *b.*–116: Silver Burdett. 116–117: © 1984 George Hall/Woodfin Camp & Associates. 117: © Harald Sund. 120–121: Olivia Cole.

Chapter 7 122–123: R. Mahoney/Bruce Coleman. 124: Michal Heron for Silver Burdett. 125: *l.* J. Gerard Smith; *r.* Joan Menschenfreund/Taurus Photos. 133: © Van Bucher/Photo Researchers, Inc. 134: © 1984 Dick Durrance II/Woodfin Camp & Associates. 135: *t.* Paul Conklin; *b.* National Park Service/Photo by Fred Bell. 136: *t.l.* Michal Heron; *t.r.* Dirck Halstead/Gamma-Liason; *b.* Raoul Hackel/Stock, Boston. 137: *t.l., t.r.* Silver Burdett; *m.* John Lei/Stock, Boston; *b.l.* Charles Harbutt/Archive Pictures, Inc.; *b.r.* Owen Franken/Stock, Boston. 138: *t.* © Harald Sund; *b.* Dr. E. R. Degginger. 138–139: Dirck Halstead/Gamma-Liason. 139: *l.* Phil Degginger; *r.* © William Bacon III/Photo Researchers, Inc. 140: *t.l.* Phil Degginger; *t.r.* © David Krasnor/Photo Researchers, Inc.; *b.* Ellis Herwig/Stock, Boston. 141: *t.* Russel Thompson/Taurus Photos; *b.* Lee Foster/Visualeyes. 142: *t.* John Running; *b.* Phil Degginger. 142–143: © Kinsler/Photo Researchers, Inc. 143: *l.* Edith G. Haun/Stock, Boston; *r.* © Dick Rowan/Photo Researchers, Inc. 144: *t.* Werner Stoy/Camera Hawaii. *b.* © Harald Sund. 145: Werner Müller/Peter Arnold, Inc. 150–151: Rosalyn Schanzer.